The Benefits of Brexit

Henry Becket

Published by New Generation Publishing in 2023

Copyright © Henry Becket 2023

First Edition

The author asserts the moral right under the Copyright, Designs and Patents Act 1988 to be identified as the author of this work.

All Rights reserved. No part of this publication may be reproduced, stored in a retrieval system or transmitted, in any form or by any means without the prior consent of the author, nor be otherwise circulated in any form of binding or cover other than that which it is published and without a similar condition being imposed on the subsequent purchaser.

ISBN: 978-1-80369-924-0

www.newgeneration-publishing.com

New Generation Publishing

Apology

The author wishes to apologise for the dearth of positive findings about the benefits of Brexit in the pages which follow. Try as he might, over the course of seven years he couldn't find a single thing.

Acknowledgements

To my "remainer friends" as well as my remaining friends (you know who you both are), and to my family, including my wife Philippa, daughter Sophie and brother-in-law Robert Thackery, for their help and encouragement in this seminal work, which – given the vast volume of research and writing/rewriting involved – necessitated my seclusion from everyday life for an unconscionable time.

By the same author

The Becket List: An A to Z of First World Problems
(Red Door, 2020)

The Becket List II: Even More First World Problems
(E-Book Partnership, 2023)

The Turbulent Past of a Little Piece of Paradise: A History of the Charente-Maritime
(New Generation , 2023)

Contents

ABOUT THE AUTHOR

Henry Becket is the author of several books both humorous and sensible, as well as innumerable utterly unmemorable TV commercials. His qualifications for this important work include a combination of being able to take things both very seriously and very unseriously at the same time – for which a long career in adland admirably fitted him.

Perhaps more importantly in this context he has always seen himself as a European and not a Little Englander, an experience begun by working on the original referendum campaign in 1975. Like many, he was devastated by the result of the 2016 referendum, which is increasingly seen – even by some of its proponents and believers – to be an error of historic proportions.

The premise of his book is that, however hard you search, it is nigh-on impossible to uncover a shred of evidence, even after all these years, that Brexit was a good thing – let alone the ghastly version with which we have been lumbered.

www.ingramcontent.com/pod-product-compliance
Ingram Content Group UK Ltd.
Pitfield, Milton Keynes, MK11 3LW, UK
UKHW041845200726
13854UKWH00005BA/2074